Breaking the Darkness

By Craig B. Cooper

ISBN 978-1-257-82332-1

www.craigbcooper.com

Published by Craig B. Cooper

Preface

God wants you free and walking in the light!

Luke 4:18-19 "The Spirit of the Lord is on me, because he has anointed me to preach good news to the poor. He has sent me to proclaim freedom for the prisoners and recovery of sight for the blind, to release the oppressed, to proclaim the year of the Lord's favor."

The devil wants to put you into bondage and darkness!

Acts 26:18a to open their eyes and turn them from darkness to light, and from the power of Satan to God,

"Breaking the Darkness" was written to help identify where the devil has brought darkness into our lives and show the path of how to be filled with God's light. It is not enough to just break the bondage of the devil's darkness in your life. You have to also be filled with the light of God to stay free.

This booklet is by no means a comprehensive study of any of these subjects. It is a condensed booklet that will 'jumpstart' your understanding of these dark areas. As you apply the basic information in this book the Holy Spirit will lead you to more information if you need it. Be blessed and break free from darkness!

Table of Contents

Part 1 - Control

Part 2 - Rejection

Part 3 - Poverty

Part 1

CONTROL

1

What is a Control Spirit?

Rev. 2:20 Nevertheless, I have this against you: You tolerate that woman Jezebel, who calls herself a prophetess. By her teaching she misleads my servants into sexual immorality and the eating of food sacrificed to idols.

In the last days we need to be on the lookout for a woman called Jezebel. Is this a real woman with the name of Jezebel? No, it is a type and shadow of a person that will be in the church that calls herself a prophetess. This verse gives us a few clues as to her behavior. But we need to realize that this type of person has been around a long time.

The name of Jezebel comes from the wife of King Ahab in the Old Testament.

1 Kin. 16:29-31 [29]In the thirty-eighth year of Asa king of Judah, Ahab son of Omri became king of Israel, and he reigned in Samaria over Israel twenty-two years. [30]Ahab son of Omri did more evil in the eyes of the LORD than any of those before him. [31]He not only considered it trivial to commit the sins of Jeroboam son of Nebat, but he also married Jezebel daughter of Ethbaal king of the Sidonians, and began to serve Baal and worship him.

Queen Jezebel was a mean, devil worshipping, controlling queen that hated God and tried to destroy everything that represented God. We know from history that sex was one of her primary weapons to control men to get her way. If that didn't' work she would then kill her enemies.

1 Kin. 18:4 While Jezebel was killing off the LORD'S prophets, Obadiah had taken a hundred prophets and hidden them in two caves, fifty in each, and had supplied them with food and water.)

The demonic spirit that drove Jezebel to act the way she did has become known as the spirit of Jezebel. The Bible does not directly call a demonic spirit this name. But Jezebel is a good example of how this particular demonic spirit uses people that give themselves to its control.

Let's define some phrases. The spirit of Jezebel is also called the spirit of control. It was the demonic spirit of control that was using the person Jezebel. That is why you will often hear the phrase a Jezebel spirit. Please note that the Jezebel spirit can operate in men or women. It is not limited to one gender.

Goal of a Control Spirit

There is one clear goal of the demonic spirit of control. That goal is to destroy everything that is being controlled or used by God and put itself in control. It wants to steal your ministry, inheritance, and destiny. It will stop at nothing to accomplish this. It is a ruthless diabolical spirit.

This spirit can exert itself through people in businesses, families, churches, and civic organizations. You will find this spirit wherever there are people and an agenda to control. This chapter discusses how this control spirit infiltrates, takes over, and controls in the church.

The spirit of control is a very strong spirit and is not easily defeated. It takes a combination of deliverance, renewing the mind with the Word, and a changing of behavior in many areas of life. It takes great effort to learn to stop being in control and let the Holy Spirit guide you and your actions.

In a church this spirit first targets and tries to neutralize all who live fervent Christianity by substituting something else, a new truth, or a false plan for their love for Jesus.

Once a church or a people are in the control of a Jezebel it is a form of slavery. The people are no longer free to follow Jesus. They substitute relying on the Holy Spirit for relying on a person who has a false agenda.

As the end times get closer we know that the power of God will be stronger and His people will do great exploits for Him. Just as God is bringing forth a new breed of prophetic people in the earth, the devil is bringing forth a counterfeit group. In the last days Jezebel will be the church's greatest enemy. She will again be trying to kill prophetic people just like Queen Jezebel of old.

2

Signs of a Control Spirit

These signs are typical signs of someone who wants to dominate and control. Keep in mind that just because someone may exhibit one or two of these behaviors does not mean they are being influenced by a demonic spirit. These are only typical signs and you have to judge by the spirit and other signs what their motivations are. This list is only used as a reference point to help in your discernment.

The best way to use this list is to compare your own heart against it. It is very important that we don't try to control or manipulate others, even if we think we are doing God's will.

In Personal Life

- Confusion. Caused by witchcraft prayers and manipulation.

- Insecurity. Causes you to constantly ask the question, "Am I really doing what I am supposed to do?" The Jezebel spirit does not want you to find your place and mature because then you wouldn't need them any longer.

- Constantly changing opinions by the Jezebel. The spirit of control wants to keep you off balance so that you constantly need them.

- Drained. Emotional, physically, and spiritually. It is spiritual warfare that affects your whole body.

- Compromise. You find yourself doing things just to make people happy and leave you alone. These are things that you would never do if the other person wasn't around.

- Strife, Division, People being stirred up. The goal is to divert people from their primary assignment in the Lord. The end result is no peace often resulting in anger.

1 Kings 21:25 There was never a man like Ahab, who sold himself to do evil in the eyes of the LORD, urged on by Jezebel his wife.

- Are strings attached to things given to you or acts done for you? If so you are being controlled through their "generosity".

- Are you supported and loved only as long as you don't disagree? If so affection is being given as payment for following them.

In Church

- You may be being controlled if:

    - You hear, "You do not acknowledge my gifting".

    - People want your gift/ministry for their agendas not for what is best for you. This can be shown if you step down for a time or take a sabbatical. Do people get aggravated, even mad at you? This means they care more about what you do for them than who you are.

    - People want to spend more time with them than is reasonable.

    - You hear, "My last pastor did not know how to use or relate to me"

- False teaching and prophecies. Jezebels love the positions of teacher and prophet because they can control through the false information given out.

- People are not being set free to follow God but to follow a person or ministry. Jezebels want people to cling to them and not God.

- There is some sign or evidence that they are more spiritual than you. But of course, in the end, only a select few ever manage to get there.

- Legalism or special rules are created. The rules created are based on what they think the people will accept. The rules sound spiritual but in effect are based on performance and not grace.

Rev. 2:24 Now I say to the rest of you in Thyatira, to you who do not hold to her teaching and have not learned Satan's so-called deep secrets (I will not impose any other burden on you):

- The Jezebel spirit is often found around money trying to manipulate events to their favor.

- People can't hear the meat of the word. They often go to sleep or get a blank look on their face.

- Immediately upon arrival into your group they give awesome dreams, visions, prophecies, or latest teaching that is the new revelation. Usually the dreams and revelations are made up and not from God.

- Wear out the saints – especially the leaders – so that they can be in control.

- Very independent spirit. They need no one unless they will bring them something in gaining power, position, or pre-eminence.

- Critical and judgmental, but not in an overt way. Done in a very subversive manner in order to discredit authority and the vision.

- Feeds on Information for the purpose of manipulation later. This is the life blood of a Jezebel. This is why they love gossip in the name of ministry.

In Family

- Someone else is ruling your household that shouldn't be.
- Relatives want to know everything going on.
- One spouse holding back another spouse from their calling in the name of something noble. They are desiring to thwart your gift or use it all up at home.
- One spouse never really cleaving to the other in true intimacy.
- A member always trying to get you to gratify your flesh when you move out in prayer or something for God. This could be sex, food, television, sleep, etc.
- Jezebel means "without co-habitation". Those with this spirit are very difficult to live with or be with.

Characteristics of a Control Spirit

- Wants Authority. This is why they target leaders. They don't mind power and control thru others.
- Back Stabber. Flatter you then talk about you behind your back.
- Self-Serving. All about them.
- Politically Correct/Chameleon in Public.
- Domineering.
- Possessive.
- Controls through the use of their personality and intimidation.
- Steals, Kills, and Destroys.

3

Strategy in the Church

The devil desperately wants to be in control of a church or ministry. It fears the power of a church that is fully submitted to the Holy Spirit. It will do anything to keep people from walking with the Holy Spirit. It will try everything to insert itself between God given leadership and the Head of the Church Jesus. The Holy Spirit was sent to the church by the Jesus to help guide us as to God's will. The demonic spirit will do everything it can to take the Holy Spirit's place. It does not come as a dark evil force. But it disguises itself as an angel of light to deceive you and lead you astray.

2 Cor. 11:13-14 For such men are false apostles, deceitful workmen, masquerading as apostles of Christ. And no wonder, for Satan himself masquerades as an angel of light.

Here are some typical steps that someone motivated by their own agenda and desire to control may follow to infiltrate a church.

1. Target Leadership

- Infiltrate leadership as fast as possible.
- A red flag is when they want to only talk to the top person

2. Get a Position

- Jezebel wants a position of authority not one of service. Inquires about leadership positions not positions that are 'behind the scenes'.
- Wants to be seen, does not like the shadows.
- Especially likes to be in charge of intercession, prophetic ministry, teaching, or counseling. Areas where there is interaction with people that they can start controlling with words or advice.

3. Create Soul Ties

- The Jezebel person is very clever. They gain entry into your life primarily through your emotions. They do this through a place where you have let them in.
- By manipulating emotional hurts, wounds, and discontentment through the following people:
    - The rebellious are targeted and manipulated through their rebellion against legitimate authority.
    - The weak/wounded by promising them help where they have been

hurt.

    - Those being disciplined/corrected by God with the thought being planted that God is doing you wrong.

- Build a following for leverage later.

- Always operate in a crisis mode. “We have to deal with this now!”

4. "Flows" in Personal Prophecy and Teaching

- Out to steal the mantle of revelation. "Godly" revelation will increase when leader is gone.

- Words and teachings designed to feed pride or justify how you were wronged.

- “The Lord showed me something about you….” The word may be accurate but the motivation is wrong.

- "I sense people here don't really understand your calling."

5. Starts Private Ministry – Preferably within the Church

- Pulls people off to the side.

- Starts a "more anointed" cell group or Bible Study.

- Starts something with a "super spiritual" atmosphere.

- Then seeds fear - "something is wrong here at church but I don't quite have it all yet, would you pray with me?"

6. Seek and Manipulate Information to Perpetuate Position

- Lots of It.

- Don't give them any!

- Will try to get all ‘parts’ to come through them so that they can manipulate and control the flow of information.

4

How a Control Spirit Approaches You

Realize that this spirit in the person wants to control you or circumstances. Remember that we are fighting against the demonic influence and not the person. Don't battle in the flesh. Battle with the weapons of the Spirit. This is the only way that you can get free and possibly get the other person free too.

Ephesians 6:12 For our struggle is not against flesh and blood, but against the rulers, against the authorities, against the powers of this dark world and against the spiritual forces of evil in the heavenly realms.

This spirit first approaches you to gain control in one of three methods: Seduction, Manipulation, or Intimidation. Usually the spirit will approach you first through seduction followed by manipulation if the seduction fails. If both of those methods fail the final approach is direct intimidation.

1. Seduction

- Insincere Compliments.
- Flattery, Smooth Words.
- Says things like, "You're so wonderful. No one prophecies like you do. No one understands you like me." Absalom used this method to try and overthrow his father David.
- Sexual Overtones in their actions and words.

Note: Beware of people who never correct you.

2. Manipulation

- Silent Treatment.
- Pouting.
- Crying.
- Creating Uncomfortable Atmosphere.
- Unpredictable Responses – Live in fear of how they will react.

If these two methods don't work then Jezebel comes at you directly through intimidation. When it has gotten to this stage this means the spiritual warfare is open and it is all out war. The battle is full blown and one of you will have to give in or die for a resolution to come about.

3. Intimidation

1 Kings 19:2 So Jezebel sent a messenger to Elijah to say, "May the gods deal with me, be it ever so severely, if by this time tomorrow I do not make your life like that of one of them."

The controller will says things like, "This will happen to you if you don't...", or "You will not be blessed if..." or "If you leave you will not be blessed." or "You will be a failure." or "You can't do it without me."

They will talk and gossip about you to others. They may even threaten you.

A common method of control to force you to do what they want is to try to circle the wagons around you to isolate you. Convert your friends and advisors. Try to get others to agree with them against you.

If you don't respond then they give you a rebuke.

Please note that seduction, manipulation, and/or intimidation precedes control. If you don't contend with these things you will end up being controlled. If you try to make 'peace' with it you may achieve external peace for a time but it will put you in bondage in the end.

5

How Do You Defeat a Control Spirit?

The chapter heading would be more accurate if we asked the question, "How do you keep a control spirit from influencing you?" We cannot actually defeat a control spirit in someone else if they want that spirit to operate in their life. But we can defeat it in the sense that its effect on us is minimized. Here are some steps to follow to do that. Keep in mind that you will have to apply these steps to your own particular circumstances. Not all steps will apply to every situation.

1. Test - Spirits/Words/Teachings, etc.

Someone operating in a control spirit will often use 'words from God' to get their way. It is important that everything be judged by 2 or 3 witnesses. This includes your own internal confirmation that the word is from God. If you don't have witness with the word discard it or at the very least put it on a 'shelf' to be confirmed in another way in the future.

1 John 4:1 Dear friends, do not believe every spirit, but test the spirits to see whether they are from God, because many false prophets have gone out into the world.

1 Thess. 5:21 Test everything. Hold on to the good.

Know those who labor among you. Be open to everybody but don't give authority or trust to someone who has not proven themselves with character over time.

I Thessalonians 5:12 (KJV) And we beseech you, brethren, to know them which labour among you, and are over you in the Lord, and admonish you;

2. Take Personal Responsibility

Repent of any involvement where you have allowed the Jezebel Spirit to control you in your life. This could even be where you gave in to the spirit because you hated conflict. Conflict is not good but giving in to the demands to keep peace gave ground to their influence.

You may need to get counseling in order to get emotional healing & deliverance from battling the control spirit in someone else. This is understandable. Seek out those who are mature and have experience in this area.

If you have been controlled you may need to deal with insecurity that makes us control or be controlled. Finally, dedicate your relationship to Jesus and the Holy Spirit to make God Lord in your life and no one else.

If you have been a controller of others you need to repent of playing the Holy Spirit in their lives. You have taken the place of God as an authority in their lives. There are many reasons we try to control others. Chapter 6 outlines some of these reasons. Go before the Lord and mature counselors to ascertain why you are doing what you are doing. You will not get totally free from the control spirit till the root problems are solved. These root problems are usually related to some fear or past abuse. We control to keep certain things from happening again.

3. Fight with Spiritual Authority, Strength, and Fortitude

You have to learn to fight. You cannot let others do the fighting for you! It is trying to control you so you must fight the battle personally. You can get strength and encouragement from others, but you have to take the actual steps to deal with the situation.

Identify where you are being stolen from and start binding up the witchcraft over your life.

Plug into a local church. Don't be a floater. This is where you will get impartation and corporate anointing to overcome.

Learn warfare prayer and tongues. You are dealing with a strong spirit. Remember that strong flesh and weak spirits will not open heavens to give you victory.

Resolve to overcome. Compromise and being average is the enemy of victory.

Rev. 2:25 Only hold on to what you have until I come.

4. Cutoff - You Cannot Make Peace

2 Kin. 9:5-7 [5]When he arrived, he found the army officers sitting together. "I have a message for you, commander," he said. "For which of us?" asked Jehu. "For you, commander," he replied. [6]Jehu got up and went into the house. Then the prophet poured the oil on Jehu's head and declared, "This is what the LORD, the God of Israel, says: 'I anoint you king over the LORD'S people Israel. [7]You are to destroy the house of Ahab your master, and I will avenge the blood of my servants the prophets and the blood of all the LORD'S servants shed by Jezebel.

The person trying to control you has to be cutoff. If you try to make peace you will lose in the end. The controlling spirit will allow you to make temporary peace if it thinks it will live another day to come back at you. Until the person gets deliverance there is no peace.

2 Kin. 9:22-24 [22]When Joram saw Jehu he asked, "Have you come in peace, Jehu?" "How can there be peace," Jehu replied, "as long as all the idolatry and witchcraft of your mother Jezebel abound?" [23]Joram turned about and fled, calling out to Ahaziah, "Treachery, Ahaziah!" [24]Then Jehu drew his bow and shot Joram between the shoulders. The arrow pierced his heart and he slumped down in his chariot..

- Be bold and aggressive. Refuse to compromise your call.
- Everything that exalts itself against God must die. The fate of Jezebel was to be eaten by dogs. 2 Kings 9:36
- Ruthless faith and militant determination is required. A nice believer will not cut it. It will take believers with "ruthless faith" who stand for Godliness and righteousness.
- Don't seek their approval. They will never totally approve. It is a trick to keep you coming back to them.
- Stop talking to them. Cut off the information flow.
- Don't let yourself be separated from other believers.
- Don't ask them to do anything for you.

If the Jezebel spirit is operating in someone within the church the following additional steps are suggested:

The following steps should be followed if you are wanting to defeat a control spirit in a local church or organization:

5. Maintain an Openness, Honesty, and Sharing Environment in the Leadership Team

The leadership team or Presbytery in a church must regularly share thoughts, insights, their 'parts', etc. with one another. Each person is given 'a part' of what God is doing and there must be an avenue where these 'parts' can be shared regularly with the whole team at the same time. A Jezebel spirit will try to get all 'parts' to come through them so that they can manipulate and control the flow of information.

The more open, transparent, and honest a leadership team can be the harder it is for a Jezebel spirit to hide and manipulate. The light of day is one of the best weapons against the deeds of darkness.

6. The Controlling Person Must Be Dealt With By the Senior Leader

Otherwise, the Jezebel will go to the senior leader after the meeting and try to out flank you.

7. Obtain Very Good Documentation of What the Person Has Done

Be ready to give an example with supporting testimony if necessary. Be specific. Approach the person and tell them what has happened. Deal with what they have done. Do not specifically say they have a controlling spirit. This will only put them on the defensive and will not accomplish anything.

8. Pray Before The Meeting That the Person Will See Their Wrong And Truly Repent

Search you own heart that you are not committing the same sin. Ask God to reveal in you any weaknesses that you have. Do not go in an attitude of pride or retribution. Go in humility and service. Your goal is restoration not punishment. But you must be firm and honest. Do not get angry but talk with a very professional matter-of-fact tone. It is important that the person repent for their behavior and not just feel sorry because they were caught. Pray for discernment to know the difference.

9. Make Sure That When You Talk To the Person That You Do Not Do It Alone

There needs to be at least two people. Otherwise, the person could twist your words and use the meeting against you. In that case it would be your words against theirs. If the person is a Jezebel and does not want to repent they could cause much chaos in a situation like this.

10. Do Not Reinstate the Person Back Into Leadership Quickly

Make sure adequate time has passed to ascertain the person's true heart and motives.

11. If the Person Is Unrepentant And Will Not Go Through Counseling You Have No Choice but to Remove Them From Leadership

Small battles produce small victories, great battles produce great victories. Dealing with a controlling spirit is a great battle that will produce a great victory. It is never fun dealing with this demonic spirit but you must be as determined and uncompromising as they are in dominating you or the church.

One last bit of wisdom – you must deal with the problem! If you ignore them hoping that it will go away it will not. It will only get worse and the longer you wait the harder it will be to remove their influence in the future.

6

Path to Operating in a Control Spirit

Why does someone operate or be used by a demonic control spirit? I don't believe anybody goes out seeking to be demonically influenced. It is usually a series of steps that 'set you' up or take you into areas that are not God. The reasons this can happen are many. But this chapter talks about one of the most common reasons people start to operating in the wrong spirit.

Keep in mind that there are other ways but this is one of the most common. This chapter talks about how a control spirit often gains entrance in someone's life who has been in abusive situations.

It generally happens in 6 steps:

Abuse -> Self-Protection -> Control ->

Witchcraft -> Personality -> Jezebel

1. Abuse

There is some form of abuse and victimization in the person's life. Out of this abuse walls of self-protection are built which try to control everything around them so that they will not be victimized again.

2. Self-Protection

The self-protection is done because the authorities that are supposed to protect the person do not. Over time this self defense mechanism allows a control spirit to come into the person's life.

3. Control

The control grows and becomes stronger. The person learns that they can protect themselves better if they actively control those around them.

4. Witchcraft

When we actively control others the Bible calls this witchcraft.

5. Personality

Over time this behavior becomes an integral part of the person and they do not know where they start and where the demonic influence starts. They have given themselves over to this controlling behavior as a habitual pattern. This behavior pattern becomes a part of their identity.

6. Jezebel

The person has become fully controlling in some areas of their lives towards others and is now considered to be a Jezebel.

Conclusion

This chapter has been on how to identify and deliver yourself from the control spirit trying to control you. It does not tell you how to deliver yourself when you have the control spirit. If after reading this chapter you discern that you have the spirit of control working in your life you will need help from mature Christians to get free from this powerful demonic spirit.

It will take counseling and accountability from a mature Christian to help you to renew your mind and develop different habits. Your personality has been greatly affected by this spirit. You will have to learn where your personality begins and where the demonic behavior begins. Your personality will have to change and become the personality that God intended for you. The spirit of control has been such a part of your personality that you will have many blind spots that you will needs others to watch out for. Nothing is too hard for the blood of Jesus and there is victory if you will walk closely with Him and other mature believers.

A summary sheet of the control spirit operating in a church is listed below. I did not write this summary sheet. Unfortunately, the author is unknown otherwise credit would be given. It is reproduced below because of its excellent summary of how the control spirit develops in a church or ministry.

Development of the Control Spirit in 7 Steps

Step	Name	Cause
1	Name: **Flattering Spirit** Symptoms: Compliments Pastor. This church is it! May compare how great you or your church is to other pastors or churches	Need for Covering
2	Name: **Super Spiritual Spirit** Symptoms: Getting lots of "words" from God during prayer. May be much fasting. Gets hold of new book or tape. Starts getting vision for church that Pastor should be getting.	Insecurity
3	Name: **Super Saint** Symptoms: May begin prophesying more and more, nearly every service. Or has to do something or say something nearly every service. Prays manipulative prayers in group intercession.	Need for Recognition
4	Name: **Competitive Spirit** Symptoms: "Deeper" than Pastor. More revelation than Pastor. New truth Pastor doesn't have. Pastor too slow. Begins to maneuver to be a leader.	Need to be in Authority
5	Name: **Jezebel Spirit** Symptoms: May interrupt Pastor or leader while teaching. Corrects Pastor in private or publicly. Sows discord among brethren, especially against leadership.	Need to Control
6	Name: **Fit of Rage** Symptoms: Won't submit to Pastor's correction or counseling. Won't admit wrong. Won't repent. Gets angry. Cries, whimpers to manipulate you to let her stay. Self-pity. Must be asked to leave.	Correction
7	Name: **Treachery** Symptoms: Attempts to convince others to leave after gone. Repeats cycle in next church.	Self-Justification

Part 2

7

Signs of Rejection

Rejection is the feeling of not being liked, accepted, loved, valued, or received. It also causes us to measure our self-worth based on others acceptance. This causes a vicious cycle downward. When we are rejected we get hurt and respond poorly. This causes others to reject us even further.

Rejection is a terrible feeling that has some of its foundations in truth but is greatly amplified by the enemy and our perceptions of the world around us. Rejection is bondage and it is very hard to break without the power of the Holy Spirit showing us the acceptance that God already has of us. It can be done but this is one enemy that we need to understand how it works so that it can be fully removed from our lives.

God loves you fully and unconditionally. He has great plans and promises for you. The enemy, often at an early age, tries to come between you and the Father's love. He tells you that you are not wanted and loved. He tells you that any love you receive from others and God is conditional upon you doing something. While this may be true with some people it is not true with God. He always loves us where we are at. If our enemy can get you to believe otherwise he is then able to cut you off from the love of God which is your only hope of salvation.

Keep in mind that just because someone may exhibit one or two of these behaviors does not mean they are being influenced by a demonic spirit. These are only typical signs and you have to judge by the spirit and other signs what their motivations are. This list is only used as a reference point to help in your discernment.

Internal Signs of Rejection

The following is a list of internal feelings that are signs that we may be plagued by the enemy in the areas of rejection.

- Feelings of worthlessness.
- Wishing you had never been born.
- Feelings of inferiority.
- Guilt.

- Feel unworthy and think God and everybody else thinks this same way.

- Thinking that God's promises are for everyone else but not us.

- Performance oriented behavior looking for acceptance in what we do.

External Signs of Rejection

The following is a list of behaviors that we exhibit outwardly towards others that can be indicative of a battle with rejection.

- Have trouble receiving love, praise, compliments from others.

- Push those who try to love them away if they get to close. Sometimes this is done in a mean and abusive way. Other times it is done by becoming aloof and withdrawn. The drawing away is done so that they will not get in a position of trust with someone and then may be rejected later. The thought of the rejection is too painful to put themselves in that position again. So they do the rejecting *first* before others can do it.

- Those with rejection *do not* appreciate those who love them. They have so many barriers that they cannot even see when people are trying to help them.

- Because of the hurt, deception comes in and rejected people often will receive help from those that are not a good influence on them. The deceiving friend's demons and the rejected person's hurts seem to find each other. In the end the rejected person is abused even more.

- Rejected people often seek out other rejected people to sympathize with them. This feels good for a little while, but in the end it reinforces the behavior. They think if they don't stay rejected then I will get no sympathy at all. It is important to find someone that will sympathize with you and love you but will help pull you up out of the wounds and hurts.

- Cannot receive correction very well. The rejected take correction as an attack against their very core personality. They cannot separate their behavior/actions from the real them. The rejected must learn that when correction is applied it restores the right things into their lives. The purpose of correction (as opposed to abuse) is to bring advancement and take us to another level beyond our current abilities. Correction is not an attack against you but your external actions.

- The rejected person has a Dr. Jeykl / Mr.Hyde personality. The real them that we are drawn too is wonderful. The rejected part with wounds and hurts is a self-centered, rude, impertinent, non-civil, and Mr. Hyde personality. They are usually touchy, overly sensitive, and avoid emotional exchanges with others. They often wear their negative feelings on their shoulders.

8

Causes of Rejection

We become rejected because we have been rejected! The enemy brings circumstances into our lives through people to hurt us and to blind us to the true unconditional love of God. His tactics are very deceitful and hurtful. Many times he will make us believe that it is even God causing this pain.

Rest assured that God did not want these hurtful things to happen to you. God has given free will to man to choose his own path and when they choose their own path it brings devastation and hurt to others. As we identify where the rejection has entered into our lives we can then bring the pain to God and He will start the healing process.

Here is a list of some of the ways that rejection comes into our lives.

- Hurts, wounds, and other pain.
- Generational curses.
- Divorce.
- Betrayal.
- Trauma.
- Abandonment.
- Neglect.
- Violated trust.
- Handicaps.
- Abuse whether physically, emotionally, or sexually.
- Lack of love from a spouse, parent, or grandparent.
- Unwanted pregnancy.
- Public humiliation.
- Failure.
- Bankruptcy.

- Poor performance academically or in sports.
- Sibling rejection.
- Betrayal by children.
- Family turmoil.

Again, realize that it was not God's will for these things to happen to you. But as we turn to Him for healing He is more than enough to help us work through the rejection, pain, and hurt. He will replace the pain with His unconditional love that will heal the deepest wound.

9

Remedy for Rejection

This chapter contains 5 thought patterns that God wants you to learn. These thought patterns are not normal for you to think if you are suffering from rejection. But these thoughts are His thoughts and as we learn to think about ourselves as He things about us it will start us on the path towards healing.

Ask the Holy Spirit regularly to help you change your old thought patterns into God's thought patterns. Give the Holy Spirit permission to point out to you where your thinking is not like God's thinking. Overtime you will find that where rejection has wound itself around your personality that the Holy Spirit is unwinding it and replacing it with love and security.

Romans 12:2 Do not conform any longer to the pattern of this world, but be transformed by the renewing of your mind. Then you will be able to test and approve what God's will is--his good, pleasing and perfect will.

1. Realize Your Wounded Rejected Personality is Not the Real You

We must realize that the 'rejected' and 'wounded' personality that we think is us is actually not us. It is a collection of hurts, wounds, disappointments on top of who the real person is. Soul pain is at the root of our inappropriate behavior towards others.

We must learn who we really are and base our actions on that and not on what others want. This takes much soul searching and conforming ourselves to what God says about us. We have spent much of our lives doing what we thought others expected of us that we don't know who we are or what we want.

2. Realize God says You are Valuable For Who You Are and Not Because of What You Do

A new way of thinking about yourself is needed that is not based on works, but rather an identity provided by God. The challenge is to do this without 'rejecting' others around us as we go through this process.

We are constantly being bombarded with opportunities to be rejected. We have to learn how to deal with the negative feelings of that rejection. We have to learn that we are valuable in God and the way that He has created us and not based on others or even our own sense of worth. It is important to not internalize the feelings and make them your own.

Even when it appears that you have been rejected or left out by someone God has not left you out. What others think about you is not as important as what God thinks about you. Our faith in God is the final anchor of everything. We need to learn that He is always a good God and we can trust Him fully. Pray for revelation and understanding of the depths of His *unconditional* love.

We must learn to exchange the feelings of rejection with the knowledge of acceptance. When we fail to accept ourselves in Jesus, rejection has an open door to our emotions! We are unconditionally loved, totally accepted, and complete in Christ.

The *antidote* for rejection is not *acceptance and approval* from others. Others cannot "love" the rejection out of you. The cure for the spirit of rejection is *sacrificing the desire for man's acceptance and approval for the acceptance and approval of God alone.*

Man's Opinion vs. God's: What is true concerning the spirit of rejection is true for all things. When we look to man for our solution (in this case, for man's acceptance and approval) we settle for a cheap imitation with no real and lasting value. When we set our face to see God alone and God only - we find our victory. The spirit of rejection is defeated. That is because there is no rejection in God for those who seek *His* face first, foremost and alone. This He promises in His Word.

Can a woman forget her sucking child, that she should not have compassion on the son of her womb? yea, they may forget, YET WILL I NOT FORGET THEE. (Isaiah 49:15).

Let your conversation be without covetousness; and be content with such things as ye have: for he hath said, I WILL NEVER LEAVE THEE, NOR FORSAKE THEE. (Hebrews 13:5)

What does it matter what man thinks of me when God has called me the apple of his eye?

Zechariah 2:8 For this is what the Lord Almighty says: "After he has honored me and has sent me against the nations that have plundered you--for whoever touches you touches the apple of his eye--

He calls me Beautiful!

Song of Solomon 2:10 My lover spoke and said to me, "Arise, my darling, my beautiful one, and come with me.

The defeat of rejection comes from the peace and contentment of finding my total identity in God alone.

3. Learn to Trust 1-2 Other People Who Have Shown they Care

We must also learn to recognize who really cares about us and is trying to love us. This usually needs to be limited to 1-2 people in the beginning. We don't need to pull away from these people but take the opportunity to learn the 'ins and outs' of a right relationship with them. We need to be open to them and listen to their advice. They can often see our behavior patterns and how to get out of them better than we can.

4. Take the Pain to God to Get Healed

You must take the pain to God and get inner healing with each one. Stored up pain will build and not go away. It will keep you from ever getting peace and will not allow you to react properly to others. Forgiving those who have hurt you is very important and is required. Deliverance is also an important key in getting free.

5. Behavioral Change is Required

Change is required to get free. We have to work hard at renewing those parts of our personality that have been damaged by the hurts and wounds. We have to learn what Godly behavior and responses are like. We have to break the repetitive patterns that have caused us to be the rude, and self-centered people that we have become. We have to learn some basic manners and people skills. You can start by being polite to others, even if you don't 'feel' like it. The golden rule is a great place to start.

The use of drugs, alcohol, fantasy, and other escape behaviors for short term relief must be stopped. Disappearing from sight and going on the woe-is-me train must stop.

Pray the Following

Lord Jesus Christ, I believe that You are the Son of God and the only way to God. You died on the cross for my sins, and You rose again from the dead. I repent of all my sins, and I forgive every other person, as I would have God forgive me. I forgive all those who have rejected me and hurt me and failed to show me love, Lord, and I trust you to forgive me.

I believe, Lord, that you do accept me. Right now, because of what you did for me on the cross, I am accepted. I am highly favored. I am the object of your special care. You really love me. You want me. Your Father is my Father. Heaven is my home. I am a member of the family of God, the best family in the universe. I am accepted. Thank You!! Thank You!!

One more thing, Lord, I accept myself the way you made me. I am your workmanship, and I thank you for what You have done. I believe that you have begun a good work in me and you will carry it on to completion. And now, Lord, I proclaim my release from any dark, evil spirit that took advantage of the wounds in my life. I release my spirit to rejoice in you. In your precious name, The Lord Jesus Christ.

Scriptures

Here are some verses to meditate on to help you understand how God thinks about you and to guide you in prayer.

Jer. 30:17 But I will restore you to health and heal your wounds,' declares the Lord, 'because you are called an outcast, Zion for whom no one cares.'

Matt. 8:17 This was to fulfill what was spoken through the prophet Isaiah: "He took up our infirmities and carried our diseases."

Isaiah 53:4 Surely he took up our infirmities and carried our sorrows, yet we considered him stricken by God, smitten by him, and afflicted.

Psalms 147:2-3 The Lord builds up Jerusalem; he gathers the exiles of Israel. He heals the brokenhearted and binds up their wounds.

Hebrews 4:15 For we do not have a high priest who is unable to sympathize with our weaknesses, but we have one who has been tempted in every way, just as we are--yet was without sin.

Hebrews 7:25 Therefore he is able to save completely those who come to God through him, because he always lives to intercede for them.

Hebrews 4:16 Let us then approach the throne of grace with confidence, so that we may receive mercy and find grace to help us in our time of need.

Psalms 129:4 But the Lord is righteous; he has cut me free from the cords of the wicked.

Psalms 2:3 "Let us break their chains," they say, "and throw off their fetters."

Psalms 31:1-3, 15 In you, O Lord, I have taken refuge; let me never be put to shame; deliver me in your righteousness. Turn your ear to me, come quickly to my rescue; be my rock of refuge, a strong fortress to save me. Since you are my rock and my fortress, for the sake of your name lead and guide me...My times are in your hands; deliver me from my enemies and from those who pursue me.

Psalms 71:5-7 For you have been my hope, O Sovereign Lord, my confidence since my youth. From birth I have relied on you; you brought me forth from my mother's womb. I will ever praise you. I have become like a portent to many, but you are my strong refuge.

Psalms 84:4 Blessed are those who dwell in your house; they are ever praising you. Selah

John 6:37 All that the Father gives me will come to me, and whoever comes to me I will never drive away.

Ephesians 1:6 to the praise of his glorious grace, which he has freely given us in the One he loves.

Isaiah 54:4-6 "Do not be afraid; you will not suffer shame. Do not fear disgrace; you will not be humiliated. You will forget the shame of your youth and remember no more the reproach of your widowhood. For your Maker is your husband-- the Lord Almighty is his name-- the Holy One of Israel is your Redeemer; he is called the God of all the earth.

The Lord will call you back as if you were a wife deserted and distressed in spirit-- a wife who married young, only to be rejected," says your God.

Part 3

POVERTY

10

What is a Spirit of Poverty?

It was God's will, which was shown originally in the Garden of Eden, that each man have a destiny. You still have a destiny! That has not changed. The original commandment that God gave to Adam and Eve is still valid for today.

Gen. 1:27-28 (KJV) 27 So God created man in his own image, in the image of God created he him; male and female created he them.
28 And God blessed them, and God said unto them, Be fruitful, and multiply, and replenish the earth, and subdue it: and have dominion over the fish of the sea, and over the fowl of the air, and over every living thing that moveth upon the earth.

Our destiny is to be fruitful, multiply, subdue, and take dominion over the earth. Unfortunately, we lost the power and authority to carry out our destiny when we chose to live our life the way we wanted instead of following God's way.

One of the things Jesus did on the cross was to retrieve the authority and power that we needed our destiny again. After His resurrection He gave us the power and authority that He had won so that we could once again carry out our destiny.

One of Satan's primary jobs is to keep you from obtaining your destiny. This is because part of your inheritance is to destroy him and retrieve back all his ill-gotten property from him for the kingdom of God. He knows you can do it if you wake up to the fact of who you are in God.

To keep this from happening, he convinces you that you will never get your inheritance, that what you have now is all right and is the best that you are going to get. We then resign ourselves to settling for less.

When this happens you have been stolen from. Your potential and all that comes from that in the future will never happen.

John 10:10 The thief comes only to steal and kill and destroy; I have come that they may have life, and have it to the full.

Sometimes we step out and get a victory. But quickly words of discouragement from the enemy stops us from moving out again. Words like this - "it was not realistic", "who are you to think that would happen", "it was too good to be true", "was it really worth the fight?"

If we give into these thoughts then BAM Satan has you. It's like a great big bear trap – you aren't dead – but you aren't going to move very far either! Most of the body of Christ is in bear traps – and calling it normal!

"The greatest battle is not between who you are and what you used to be, but between who you are and what you can be" - Tony Miller

The spirit of poverty steals your future destiny by getting you to take less than what God wants for you today. We call this trap the trap of a poverty mindset. By accepting a life less than what God wants for us now we lose what He has for us in the future. It is a very subtle trap because we realize things are not right, but we never realize the great destiny we are giving up because they never materialize.

If a robber comes into your house and steals your possessions you immediately know what has been stolen. But the spirit of poverty is like a time traveling robber. He is able to go five years into the future and steals your possessions that you will accumulate over the next five years. When you finally arrive in time five years later you don't realize what was stolen because you had never seen those things. But you were stolen from anyway.

Demonic spirits cannot go five years into the future and steal your destiny. Actually, they cannot steal from you at anytime. You actually steal from yourself when you agree with the demonic thoughts they place in your mind. When you agree with those thoughts you align your mindset with a thinking that is not God's. As a result the things of God that would happen if you walk with Him never materialize.

You have to have faith to walk with God. Faith is believing that what God said He would do He will do. Our destiny is not totally dependent on us. God has His part and we have our part. Our part is to believe that His words towards us will come true and obey His voice in doing what we need to do.

Heb. 11:1 Now faith is being sure of what we hope for and certain of what we do not see.

Heb. 11:6 And without faith it is impossible to please God, because anyone who comes to him must believe that he exists and that he rewards those who earnestly seek him.

The poverty mindset is a mindset that keeps us from walking in the *fullness of God's purpose and inheritance for our life.*

This mindset will try to make you poor in all areas of life. It does not just apply to money and finances. It applies to all of the things that God wants us to walk in. It keeps you from ever having a great purpose in your life! God wants you fulfilled with His plans.

Here is a list of some of the thought patterns that are not faith that the Devil tries to get us to agree with. When we agree with these thought patterns it makes it extremely hard for God to prosper us in the areas that we have these thoughts. It means we have succumbed to a poverty mindset that has been inspired by demonic thoughts. There may even be a need for deliverance from demons that have attached themselves to your behavior.

A Poverty Mindset is:

- Refusing to become what God created and destined you to be.
- Not believing that the Lord can take you into the fullness of His plan.
- Not just experiencing lack, but having a fear that you will lack.
- When you conform to your circumstances.
- Occurs when the "god of this world" causes you to forget God's ability in the midst of your circumstance.
- A voice that says, "God is not able!"
- Holds you down from having good relationships with others, "Oh, nobody likes me."
- Holds you down from having a great relationship with God, "Oh, I don't deserve it."
- Poverty is refusing to make the necessary shifts to enter into the fullness of your destiny.
- Results in constantly being stolen from.
- Steals your will to fight. You become resigned to your situation.

- When you don't realize you are even in warfare.
- Evidenced by apathy and lethargy!
- Poverty does not believe God can bring you into your destiny.
- Being satisfied with less than what God has for you. Ten of the 12 spies who went into the land said that the riches were not worth it. They would rather stay in the hot desert drinking water & eating manna, then go into a green land & have a full banquet. Only two spies obtained their full destiny. The Israelites were in a bear trap – they were satisfied with less!
- Is refusing to move forward.
- Believes that God can't bring you through to the next level.

This is one of the most powerful and deadly strongholds that Satan uses to keep the world in bondage. We must learn to identify and overcome it if we are going to walk as overcoming Christians.

Definition of Prosperity

We need to define prosperity which is the opposite of poverty. It is important to have a biblical definition of prosperity or else we will think that it is God's will for us all to be millionaires. Prosperity is simply this – having enough of whatever you need to do God's will for your life. This includes money, time, friends, or other resources needed to carry out God's will for your life.

Prosperity is not how much can we accumulate for ourselves, but doing His will and being a channel of blessing to others.

Eph. 4:28 He who has been stealing must steal no longer, but must work, doing something useful with his own hands, that he may have something to share with those in need.

Prosperity is receiving the grace of the Holy Spirit to enable you to accomplish what you are called to accomplish. This includes a stewardship plan. A stewardship plan is where you determine ahead of time what you are going to do with the resources that God gives you. The more you steward your gifts and prosperity properly, the more you will get. This is not just a money issue! God is looking for people who will be good stewards so He can release more into their lives to bring about His will in the earth.

11

How Does Poverty Trap Us?

Poverty can occur through various means. Here are a few of the most common ways that a poverty mindset can occur. Remember that poverty is simply accepting less than what God has in mind for us in some area of our life. So many things can trigger this in our life.

1. The number one way that poverty comes into our life is not obeying the Holy Spirit. When we ignore the Holy Spirit we are not getting the instructions we need on how to walk. Many Christians actually even resist the Holy Spirit. If you resist the Holy Spirit you negate the blessing of the Lord.

2. Poverty can occur if we have a mentality of covetousness or gluttony. This includes our not wanting to share our lives and possessions with others. We become focused on ourselves. This goes against God's mindset of generosity so He stops the flow of blessings coming to our life in that area.

Prov. 23:21a for drunkards and gluttons become poor

Prov. 28:22 A stingy man is eager to get rich and is unaware that poverty awaits him.

3. Poverty can occur if we are lazy. It takes work, wisdom, and persistence to overcome our circumstances to achieve the destiny that God wants. It is not just handed to us.

Prov. 24:33-34 [33]A little sleep, a little slumber, a little folding of the hands to rest—[34]and poverty will come on you like a bandit and scarcity like an armed man.

4. Haste leads to poverty. This occurs when we fall into *"get rich quick"* schemes or try to take short cuts in the character training God is taking us through. Prosperity is not achieved overnight.

5. Poverty can occur when we live in fear and not faith. Fear is not an emotion of God. It causes us to choose the easiest way in the short term. Faith enables us to make Godly decisions based on the future.

6. Poverty can occur when we are unwilling to face the challenges and enemies in our lives.

Prov. 22:13 The sluggard says, "There is a lion outside!" or, "I will be murdered in the streets!"

7. Poverty can occur when we are persecuted in some way and we take on a victim mentality. This persecution can be for our faith, looks, actions, etc. If you have been persecuted, then your faith may be broken. You have to move back up in your level of faith.

If you have lost a war in some area there is a reproach that can make you a permanent victim in your thinking. It takes renewed faith to rise back up. We can't stop persecution but we don't have to succumb to it.

How have you dealt with your losses? We could be reacting to promises wrong because of the losses we have had.

2 Cor. 6:9 known, yet regarded as unknown; dying, and yet we live; beaten, and yet not killed;

Persecution when placed in God's hands becomes a blessing!

Matt. 5:10 Blessed are those who are persecuted because of righteousness, for theirs is the kingdom of heaven.

8. Poverty occurs when we start begging for things. Begging is thinking people are our source. Genesis 45 is the only Old Testament reference to poverty outside of Proverbs. Joseph was anointed to keep the people from experiencing poverty. In New Testament there were two concepts of poverty: begging and alms! The Lord is breaking the power of begging in His people. He is making us a people of faith. He will change the identity of His people from beggars to kings.

9. Poverty occurs when we fail to make plans of what we will do when our dreams and prosperity come true. We have to ask the question of what do we plan on doing when prosperity comes our way? Most people never plan for their dreams to come true. So usually what happens is that when prosperity comes their way they squander it on themselves.

God will never give us what we need if it is just going to go into a black hole called self. The enemy already has devised a plan to eat up your assets and returns. So we need to counter his plans with plans of our own. With Gideon, the Midianites always stole the harvest right when it came in (Judges 6). We can plant. We can watch our crops grow. We can even have breakthrough. But if we do not take time to understand how to gather and steward the spoils a strategy of poverty will begin to develop against us. When you increase without developing the storehouse to contain your spoils, the enemy will gain access to your excess and your future. We have to manage the increase or we will lose the increase. What is your plan for increase?

For instance, most people are blessed with enough finances from God. But they do not have a disciplined lifestyle of budget and savings so whenever they get more it immediately goes to something that has very little value. We have to learn how to hold what we are given so that we don't waste the blessings of God. Be a steward of your time, strength, and energy. This is a guide of how you will prosper.

10. Poverty can occur from oppression through authoritative structures. If you live under an authoritative structure (parents, civil, church, etc) that is abusive and misuses their power it will affect your own life negatively. Much wisdom and mercy from God must be received to be able to exit or change this situation.

11. Poverty mindset is passed down through our blood line or families. If our families are affected by a poverty mentality then almost always we think the same way because we do not know what the right way is.

12
How to Break Poverty

There are two areas of thought that we want to discuss that you must adopt to get rid of the poverty mindset. These two areas of thought are absolutely needed because they are central to what God wants to do in your life. These thoughts help reverse a poverty mindset.

1. God Is Not Mad At You or Sad At You, God Is Glad Over You!

Most people, especially those who have been in church, have a wrong view of God! Most people think God is mad or sad at them – they live this way. They think He is out to get you at the first opportunity possible. This is one reason people rely on their own plans instead of listening to God's plans. They don't trust God. Rest assured, He is not looking for some way to get you.

Jer. 19:11 For I know the plans I have for you," declares the Lord, "plans to prosper you and not to harm you, plans to give you hope and a future.

Also, many times we think God loves us based on what we do. But that is not true either! If we don't do the right things He is not mad at you. This is a behavior that we learned from somebody around us like a parent or some other authority figure in our life that acted this way towards us.

Others tend to think that God is sad over you because of what we have or have not done. Again, God's attitude towards us is not based on what we do. He is a God who unconditional loves us because we are His! He loved us even before we were born and able to do anything!

Did you know you are enjoyed by God? He likes being around you – He enjoys you. You don't have to wait till you are perfect in heaven before He enjoys you!

Rom. 2:4 Or do you show contempt for the riches of his kindness, tolerance and patience, not realizing that God's kindness leads you toward repentance?

2. What Jesus did on the Cross gave us all Authority

Most people misunderstand what happened at the Cross and how it changed everything! He reversed everything that sin had brought into the world in the Garden of Eden. Before sin there was no death, no sickness, no poverty and no heartache.

We do have salvation from Hell because of the Cross, but we have so much more. Because of His death He can now give us the authority to help us to reverse all of the effects of sin. Take some time and meditate on this wonderful truth!

How to Break Poverty in Your Life

We have to think from a different perspective – a heavenly perspective. We need to learn to think from a faith dimension and not a fear dimension. There is a work we have to do here on earth in order to walk in prosperity. It is not all up to God. He cannot work through a person who is working against him by following principles He does not endorse. There is always a component we have to do and a component He has responsibility for.

There are four things we must walk in to break poverty in our life in whatever area we are afflicted.

1. Repentance
2. Wisdom
3. Obedience
4. Persistence

As we walk in these four areas for the part of our life that is being robbed from we will see improvement and prosperity come.

REPENTANCE + WISDOM + OBEDIENCE + PERSISTENCE = PROSPERITY

These are general principles that need to be applied to every area of your life from which you are being stolen. You could be stolen from in your relationships, promotions at work, finances, etc. Every area that needs it we need to pray for repentance, wisdom, obedience, and persistence to carry out the plans He gives us.

1. Repentance

There are 3 steps for total repentance:

1. Repent of our behavior
2. Renounce the spirit of poverty
3. Change

First, we must first repent of the behavior that has encouraged the devil to rob you. This may be for living for us, spending all of our money on ourselves, feeling sorry for ourselves, not listening to the Holy Spirit, etc.

We have to take personal responsibility for our behavior. If we think it is somebody else's problem we will not get freedom. The first step of freedom is to assume responsibility for our part.

We need to repent for believing that God isn't big enough to solve our problems.

Deut. 8:17-19 [17]You may say to yourself, "My power and the strength of my hands have produced this wealth for me." [18]But remember the LORD your God, for it is he who gives you the ability to produce wealth, and so confirms his covenant, which he swore to your forefathers, as it is today. [19]If you ever forget the LORD your God and follow other gods and worship and bow down to them, I testify against you today that you will surely be destroyed.

We need to repent of the following things if we have believed them:

- Repent of refusing to become what God created and destined you to be.
- Repent of not believing that the Lord can take you into the fullness of His plan.
- Repent of not just experiencing lack, but having a fear that you will lack!
- Repent of conforming to your circumstances.
- Repent of passivity and apathy.

Second step of repentance is to renounce the spirit of poverty and the effect that it has on our life. It is as simple as entering into prayer with God and renouncing it. You can't stay in agreement with poverty and lack. Poverty believes that God is not able!

Third, we must be willing to change! Declare this to the Lord and to the heavens with your very own words. Openly say, "I am going to change now! My behavior will not stay the same with your help!"

The Church is in an incredible season of change. We need to believe that the Lord will come again and break you out of old cycles. Ask Him to allow you to experience His glory.

Sometimes these things are generational and take time to change. But the power and blood of the Cross can do it!

2. Wisdom

After we repent we have to change. If we keep doing the same things we have always done we will keep getting the same things we have always got!

The question is what and how do we change? This part will take some time, research, knowledge, and wisdom. The first step is to go to the Word of God and the Holy Spirit and say what needs to be changed? Then we need to get instructions on what He wants us to change to.

This is also where more mature Christians, Godly books, etc. can give us advice. If we are being stolen from in our relationships seek someone out that has good relationships. Learn from them. Buy books on how to develop good relationships. Continually pray to the Holy Spirit on why people reject you and why your relationships don't turn out good.

It is very important to realize that prosperity DOES NOT JUST HAPPEN! It is a result of repenting of old behavior, wisdom for new behavior, obedience to that wisdom, and persistence in following that wisdom.

A key component of the last 3 steps is getting the wisdom of what to change and what to change it to.

We must develop the skills and knowledge to overcome. You have to have a plan to reverse the poverty that we opened the door to.

2 Tim. 2:15 Do your best to present yourself to God as one approved, a workman who does not need to be ashamed and who correctly handles the word of truth.

Develop skill, understanding, get resources, training, etc. to fulfill your purpose. For instance, many people have a spirit of poverty attached to their finances. This could be because of many different reasons including: debt, not tithing, overspending, cosigning a loan, etc. The Bible has many guidelines on how we are to handle our finances. When we don't follow these we don't prosper.

Eccl. 10:10 If the ax is dull and its edge unsharpened, more strength is needed but skill will bring success.

Seek the Lord as to how to get out of your situation. You got into it one step at a time, God will help you get out of it one step at a time.

Beware of the enemy's schemes to steal from you. Success is the power to adapt to every circumstance to gain victory. Success occurs when we behave wisely and act prudently. Success occurs when you meditate on God's plan for your life and follow it.

3. Obedience

It goes without saying that we have to obey the wisdom that the Holy Spirit gives us.

James 1:23-25 [23]Anyone who listens to the word but does not do what it says is like a man who looks at his face in a mirror [24]and, after looking at himself, goes away and immediately forgets what he looks like. [25]But the man who looks intently into the perfect law that gives freedom, and continues to do this, not forgetting what he has heard, but doing it—he will be blessed in what he does.

4. Persistence

Persistence is continually obeying the wisdom that we receive. Success is not one big decision made correctly but lots of little decisions made correctly over time.

Part of the persistence is being willing to fight and war against our old behaviors and for where we want to go. We have to be like the 2 spies who emphasized the promise and not the Giants. It's sad that only

Joshua and Caleb went into the promise land. But they were willing to fight the giants to get it. They were and did!

We must be willing to press through difficulty and storms and force an atmospheric change. Many in the body are afraid to war. But war is necessary to take possession of what has been promised to you.

Rest assured that God will be with you and you will receive grace and the necessary armor.

Rev. 3:21 To him who overcomes, I will give the right to sit with me on my throne, just as I overcame and sat down with my Father on his throne.

The Lord brought His people out of Egypt by armies (*Ex. 12:51*) with a trumpet sound and a battle cry. He brought them out with the Ark which symbolizes the presence of God (*1 Sam. 4:5-6*). God will also go out with you when we move forward.

God will never forsake you as you pursue the right thing. He even uses forces of nature when necessary to defeat their enemies (*Josh. 10*). He always releases strategies enabling us to plunder, prosper and stand (*Matt. 10, Eph. 6*).

He has a banner of victory for you. While Jehovah-Nissi puts a banner over you to cover you, the Lord will send the Hosts of Heaven to help you. He is God of the armies of Earth (*1 Sam. 17:26*) and God of the unseen armies of angels (*1 Kings. 22:19).* He already has victory for you if you will fight!

Final Thoughts on Breaking Poverty

God is not a vending machine. All of God's promises come in 3 stages – sowing, waiting, and then reaping. We need wisdom in what and how to sow. We then have to exercise obedience and persistence during the waiting. Finally the reaping comes. The challenge is to persevere through the waiting.

Purposes of Waiting

1. Testing – Will you stand on what you know is true? Will you choose to believe the promise?

2. Warfare – Will you walk in fear and hopelessness or will you take your thoughts captive?

3. Refining – Time to learn and be taught new things and skills to prosper in the next round.

God will show Himself strong to you in the waiting.

What is Victory?

Victory is when you accomplish God's will for your life! To do that you have to struggle against difficulties and obstacles that are impeding you from overcoming. It is preserving until we get in the right place and position that God has for us. God will give you the power to adapt to every circumstance so that you can bring forth His plan (*Deut. 8:18*) for your life!

About the Author

Craig is married to Susan Luhrman Cooper; a proud Father to Abigail, Grace, and Israel; a Software Developer; and Founder/Pastor of Relationship Church.

You can get more information about the author, his family, blogs, Church, books, articles, etc. at *www.craigbcooper.com.*

Other Books by Craig

Can Women Minister to Men?

Breaking the Darkness Over Control, Rejection, and Poverty

How to Walk with the Holy Spirit

Faith Fiction

How to Be a Religious Demon

www.ingramcontent.com/pod-product-compliance
Ingram Content Group UK Ltd.
Pitfield, Milton Keynes, MK11 3LW, UK
UKHW041919190726
13854UKWH00003B/1336